Level B – Book 1
Red Herrings Science Mysteries

Solving Mysteries through Critical Questioning

ad hockett

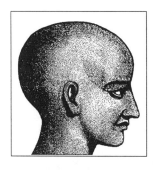

© 1996
CRITICAL THINKING BOOKS & SOFTWARE
(formerly Midwest Publications)
P.O. Box 448 • Pacific Grove • CA 93950-0448
Phone 800-458-4849 • FAX 408-393-3277
ISBN 0-89455-654-1
Printed in the United States of America

Table of Contents

About This Book

"He went to the gym with Harold and pumped iron every day, but he couldn't even lift a feather. Who was he?"

Answer: He was Harold's heart.

Red Herrings Science Mysteries uses problems like the one above to strengthen scientific and critical thinking as students play detective to find the answers. The mystery activities improve the skills of analyzing, problem solving, deductive reasoning, and synthesizing. Red Herrings allows students to exercise their reading comprehension and vocabulary skills as well as their imaginations to form a link between language arts and sciences.

The stories include "red herrings" to intentionally mislead students; as they become aware of the automatic assumptions they have made, students begin to analyze situations more effectively and objectively. Often, this is achieved by recognition of the multiple meanings of key words. Students learn to solve the mysteries as a detective would—by probing with questions and forming conclusions based upon the answers.

In addition, the activities can also reinforce and/or explore the underlying science principles. The example above is based on the following science concept:

Humans (as multicelled organisms) have organs to perform functions in the body. The heart pumps blood to make it circulate in the body. Circulating blood carries iron and other nutrients to the body parts that need them.

How It Works

Each of the "mysteries" on these pages is part of a longer untold story which is "behind the scenes." It is up to the students to deduce the rest of the story from clues derived from answers to their questions.

For example, the story behind the statement, "He may be the star of the show, but they all run circles around him" can eventually be revealed if enough questions are asked and the answers are used to form a mental image of the event. It may take many questions over several days to finally reveal that "he" is the sun and "they" are the stars in a show at the planetarium.

The Rules of the Game

The rules for the activities are simple.

- Students must phrase their questions so that the answer is either yes or no.
- Try to answer questions with only a yes or no (occasionally a *maybe* or *sometimes* can be given as an appropriate response).
- You may give hints to redirect thinking or stimulate new questions.

Behind the Scenes

The solutions to the science mysteries are found at the back of this book. It is important to visualize the scenario of the mystery before you begin a questioning session. That way you can answer questions based upon your personal mental image of what has taken place. After visualizing the scene, you may wish to alter it slightly to suit your geographic locale or your students' cultural backgrounds.

Teaching Suggestions

Although your students may be familiar with the science concept behind the mystery (they understand that the heart is an organ that pumps blood carrying iron through the body), they may find the detective process difficult at first. Don't give up! They will soon be skilled detectives having a lot of fun. You may help ease students through the initial learning process in the following ways:

- Start with a short, fun activity.
- Describe the process, using a sample problem for illustration.
- Give helpful details:
  Inanimate objects are sometimes referred to with personal pronouns. ("He" may be the earth or a gas, etc.)
  An object may be called by part of its name. (What kind of "net" did he use?— A magnet.)
- Limiting the number of questions allowed during a session tends to improve the quality of the questions.
- Choosing a student to present the story and answer the questions allows you to model inquiry techniques by taking an active part in the activity. Instead of simply describing how to formulate good questions, you can then guide the students by demonstrating higher level thinking and questioning techniques.
- It is important to summarize the clues that have already been discovered before continuing an interrupted questioning session. This refreshes students' memories and updates students who may have been absent during a questioning session. One of the best ways to review is to ask the students what they remember about the story and what clues have already been revealed.

Using These Activities

Science activity: The scientific method can be learned and reinforced through the *Red Herrings Science Mysteries* questioning process. To reinforce the scientific method, have students follow these steps for at least the first few mysteries:

- Observe: Listen to (or read) the mysteries carefully; ask questions until a hypothesis can be formed to explain the mystery.
- Form a hypothesis: Write down a reasonable explanation of the meaning of the mystery, consistent with all known clues.
- Check the hypothesis: Ask new questions that will either validate or invalidate the hypothesis.

Morning start-up activity: To get your students thinking critically right away, begin the day by presenting a science mystery.

Motivator or jumping-off point: Use the mysteries to generate curiosity about a familiar general principle before embarking on a more in-depth, detailed study.

Enrichment activity: Allow one student to act (quietly) as presenter for one or more other students, or allow students to work independently, listing possible questions for a written problem.

Cooperative activity: Students can be divided into teams. Limiting the number of questions that a team is allowed to ask keeps one group from dominating the session. Each team may ask only one question per round, and the questions may be asked only by the team's spokesperson. This helps to eliminate frivolous questions. (In fact, many students will learn quickly how to narrow the search for important clues by asking comprehensive questions.)

Another method for limiting questioning is to pass out coupons to the groups before each session. A coupon is collected before each question is answered. When the group runs out of coupons, the group is out of that questioning session.

Writing activity: You may stipulate that questions be submitted only in writing. Questions are read and answered at the beginning or end of class. To prevent students who already know the answer from spoiling the activity for others, possible solutions should also be submitted only in writing.

To develop critical listening skills: After a few practice rounds, a new rule could be imposed: repeat questions will not be answered. This causes students to listen more carefully to the questions and answers.

Critical listening and recall is improved if the students are allowed to remark (with a noise or a word) when a question is a repeat of one that has already been asked.

As a lesson in critical thinking: Like all good mystery stories, the ones in this book have vivid plots, settings, and characters. The students' questioning strategies can be improved if they look for story areas that have not been thoroughly addressed. By analyzing individual questions and suggesting ways to improve them, you can help students increase their critical thinking ability.

Using the Mystery Pages

The pages in this book are designed for multiple uses.

- Reproducing the mystery page on transparency material and using it every time the story is investigated helps students who have a limited auditory memory.
- Summarizing what the students already know about the mystery and writing it on the transparency will help those students with learning difficulties to continue to participate in the questioning activity.
- Using the mystery page as a poster in your room will serve to remind you and your students of both the activity and the mystery in progress.
- Letting everyone see the actual mystery message permits students to analyze the wording of the mystery for possible clues. You may decide that showing the words may be *too much* of a clue (as when spelling gives away the double meaning—steal, steel). In this case, you may wish to present clues verbally only.

Using Graphic Organizers

A variety of graphic organizers can be used to help students with the thinking process. Two are supplied with this text. Here are some ways they can be used.

For cooperative learning: Before beginning the questioning session, each group receives one copy of the mystery story and a copy of the graphic organizers. Encourage them to use the graphic organizers to arrange a questioning strategy. At the end of the session, the group members can map out on the organizer the direction in which the answers are leading and plan the next questioning strategies.

Modeling the thinking process: Using a transparency of Organizer #1, select a mystery and model the process of analyzing the story for clues. Are there any words in the story that could have multiple meanings? Are there any clues about the setting, characters, or action of the story? From the first reading of the mystery, what are some possible solutions?

Guided practice: Individually or in cooperative groups, students can use Organizer #1 to help them analyze the wording of a mystery story. They can contribute their ideas about the mystery before beginning the questioning session.

Summarizing: Organizer #2 can be used to list the clues that have been discovered from previous questioning sessions.

The Questioning Process

To give you a better understanding of how to use these mystery stories to develop critical thinking, here is an abbreviated script of a questioning session with a group of students.

The teacher in this example uses several strategies to get the students to think in new and different directions without giving away the premise of the story. You might want to use similar strategies with your students to get them back on track if they get stuck or start pursuing a nonproductive line of questioning.

© *1996 Critical Thinking Books & Software* P.O. Box 448 *Pacific Grove, CA 93950* (800) 458-4849 **V**

Teacher: "We're going to try to solve a science mystery today. I know the entire story behind this mystery, but I am only going to let you in on a small part of it to begin with. It will be up to you to figure out the rest of the story as a detective would, by asking good questions, listening carefully to the answers, and putting clues together to form a mental picture of what is happening.

"Here are some rules that must be followed. You may ask me any question as long as it is phrased so that my answer can be a yes or a no. Listen to the questions that others ask because you may pick up clues from my answers to their questions. Try not to repeat questions that others have already asked.

"I will attempt to answer your questions with only a yes or a no. Sometimes that is difficult to do, so I may give more than a one-word answer to some questions. Listen to the way that I answer yes or no. That may give you a clue to the solution of the mystery or help you phrase your next question.

"Do you understand the rules? If not, be sure to ask for an explanation. OK, here is the mystery story: (the teacher places the transparency of the story on the overhead or just reads to the students). It reads, 'He went to the gym with Harold and pumped iron every day, but he couldn't even lift a feather.'"

Student: "What do you mean? Is he a small guy? Is he a kid?"

Teacher: "That's what you are supposed to find out by asking questions. If you ask enough questions, you can find out exactly what is happening here. Try it. Remember, your questions must be phrased so that I can answer them with yes or no."

Student: "Was he younger than Harold? Was he older than Harold?"

Teacher: "That's two questions. I can only answer one at a time."

Student: "Was he younger than Harold?"

Teacher: "No."

Student: "How could he pump iron every day and still be so weak?"

Teacher: "I can't answer that question the way it is asked. Please rephrase the question so that I can answer it with a yes or a no."

Student: "Had he pumped iron for a long time?"

Teacher: "Yes."

Student: "By pumping iron, do you mean he lifted weights?"

Teacher: "No. That's a good question. Why do you think it is a good question?"

Student: "It eliminates a lot of things with just one question."

Student: "Do you mean pumping like a bicycle tire?"

Teacher: "Explain exactly what you mean by that kind of pumping and then I can answer you."

Student: "I mean like when you push stuff into something."

Teacher: "Yes, he pumps iron that way."

Student: "When you say 'He pumped iron…' is he a person?"

Teacher: "No. How does that question help us?"

Student: "Now we know not to ask more questions about things only a person could be doing."

Teacher: "Exactly. Could someone summarize what we know before I answer more questions?"

Student: "We know that something goes to the gym with Harold and pushes iron into something, but can't lift a feather."

Teacher: "Ask me some more questions to find out what he is and why he pumps iron."

Student: "Is he part of Harold?"

Teacher: "Yes."

Student: "Is it his arms or legs? Oh—the only other things I can think of that pump stuff are his lungs or heart."

Teacher: "Do you have a yes or no question?"

Student: "Is it his heart that pumps iron and can't lift a feather?"

Teacher: "Yes. That's it!"

Student: "Huh?"

Teacher: "Harold's heart pumps iron to the body parts that need it by causing the blood that carries iron to circulate. Of course it can't lift a feather, but there's no reason for it to do so.

"Now, do you think you understand how these mystery stories work? Well, here's another one for you to try to solve. If we don't have time to complete it today, we'll work on it when we have some time left over tomorrow or the next day."

Extending Activities

After students have experience solving the mysteries in this book, ask them to create their own stories. Sources for story ideas are mystery and science programs on television and science-related articles from magazines, books, or newspapers.

Often, the best mysteries contain words that have more than one meaning. For example, a *nail* could be a part of the finger or something to hammer. An *organ* could be a musical instrument or part of the body. Try to incorporate these kinds of words into the story.

Science Topics

The Red Herrings Science Mysteries activities are grouped according to science principles. The index on the following page provides a convenient way to locate an appropriate activity. For example, if you have recently completed a weather unit, you may find a corresponding activity by looking under EARTH SCIENCES and then Meteorology and turning to the appropriate page.

INDEX OF SCIENCE TOPICS

© 1996 Critical Thinking Books & Software   P.O. Box 448   Pacific Grove, CA 93950   (800) 458-4849

Mystery Story: _____

_____

_____

Words that have multiple meanings:

Word: _____ Meanings: _____

Word: _____ Meanings: _____

Word: _____ Meanings: _____

Word: _____ Meanings: _____

What clues can you find in the words of the mystery story?

Setting clues	Character clues	Action clues
_____	_____	_____
_____	_____	_____
_____	_____	_____
_____	_____	_____
_____	_____	_____
_____	_____	_____
_____	_____	_____

Possible Solutions:

_____

_____

_____

_____

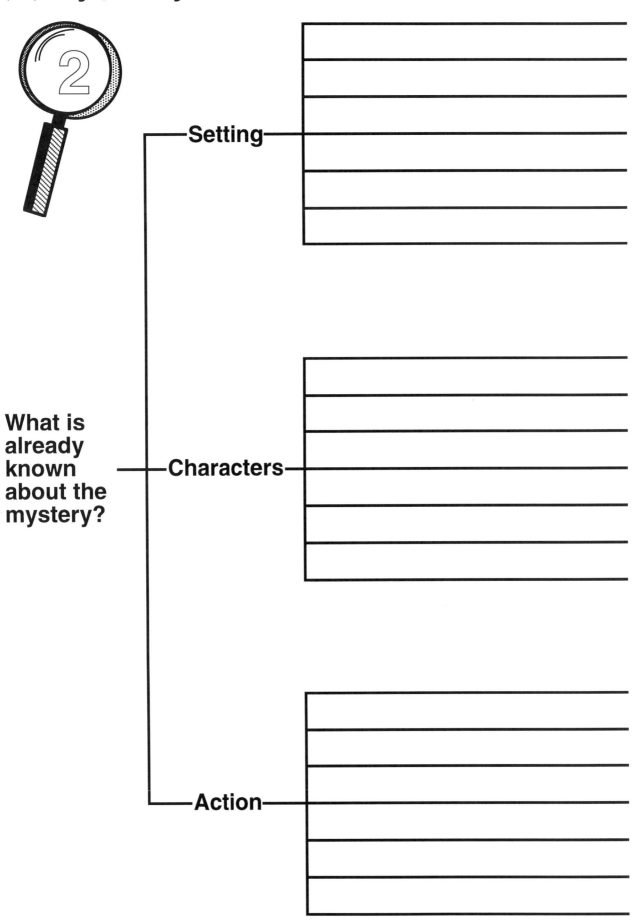

What is
already
known
about the
mystery?

Setting

Characters

Action

In our favorite movie, Capt. Bob marries several couples at sea. In one scene, however, he says, "If those two won't separate, I'll have them thrown overboard!" Who or what were those two?

They would have nothing to do with each other until a slippery character came along. Identify all three.

After going from third base to home, he didn't score and was very blue. Who or what was he?

When Zulu arrived late at the lecture hall, the professor was saying, "You can add them together in two different ways: one way results in nothing, the other results in twice as much." What was the professor talking about?

He frequently traveled by plane, but it never got off the ground. After getting off the plane, he remained in his seat. Why?

She was involved in energy conversions at the lab. She often transformed chemical energy to heat energy and then to mechanical energy, but she wouldn't tell anyone about it. Who was she?

They claimed to be using only solar energy, but we knew they burned coal and petroleum. How could this be?

Mom was cooling the house for a party and had placed a thermometer in every room. She asked Jake how much heat remained in the sunroom, but he said he had no way to tell. Why not?

Her collar had no wrinkles, but she would have to iron it or it would never be attractive. Why?

When the class needed his help, Phil resisted. The teacher put Phil at the head of the class. Why? Who or what was Phil?

Though there was no mirror, she saw her friend's reflection. Where was she looking?

He was so strong, he could bend a three-inch thick bar of iron. When he was asked to bend *this*, however, he had to call on his smaller, nearsighted friend for help. What was he asked to bend?

He went to the store to pick up a black tie. When he got home and took it out of the bag, he exclaimed, "This isn't black, it's red!" What had happened?

His pitches were perfect, with the fastest curves ever demonstrated in the ballpark. Unfortunately, his team lost the game. Why?

In science class, a message was passed to Gerald when Ms. Grayson wasn't looking. Gerald immediately revealed the message by telling the teacher out loud, "You have a lot of nerve!" She only smiled and said, "I guess we both have nerve." Who passed the message? What was going on?

He had no working
navigational panel and
was as blind as a bat, but
he made a perfect landing.
How did he navigate?

Gina and Juan each parachuted from a different plane at the same time. Though they fell in parallel lines, they became closer together as they approached the ground. Why?

It stretched out its long tail in the sun and soon disappeared. What was it?

Theresa was eating her own pie quietly when Geo suddenly pushed the plate aside violently and made a mess of both their crusts. She knew Geo was under a lot of stress, but why the violence? Who or what was Geo?

The bank deposit turned out to be a solid investment. Later, it became a liquid asset. What was the investment? What was the liquid asset?

It was only a poor rural area, but Rio took up a collection and somehow pulled contributions out of the air. Who or what was Rio? What were the contributions?

Hernandez wanted to put all the pieces of the puzzle back together, but Drifty had spread them out; now they seemed to be stuck. Who or what was Drifty, and what was the puzzle?

By running in circles at one location, X caused a collision hundreds of miles away at another location. What is the collision? Who or what is X?

The children were huddled together for warmth, but Jake said, "When they spread out, we'll feel warmer and circulation will improve." What was he talking about?

Shirley complained to the jail warden that she needed a kitchenette in her cell. "I demand equal treatment. Rosa has every necessity and can even make food right in the cell!" Why is Rosa special?

Sal refused the turkey, and Dan was embarrassed because he hadn't known that she was a vegetarian. A friend said, "You should have taken a closer look at her mouth." Why did he say that?

He was one of the most successful warriors in all the kingdoms. He had overcome much of the neighboring kingdom, but he could never force the subjects into his own kingdom. Who was he? Why couldn't he bring the subjects into his kingdom?

They failed to adhere
to regulation when
they allowed excessive
production at the factories;
therefore, they were
executed. Who or what
were they? Who executed
them?

Breaking the code will allow him access to the family fortune. Though he will inherit plenty of gold and silver, he may never be rich. Who is he? What is the code, and what is the inheritance?

Although they left detailed clues as to their whereabouts, the best detectives could never take them alive. Who or what were they?

She was chained down
and eaten by her food.
What was going on?

In the physics club, they had made fun of his spelling. Later, he wrote, "It happened a long time ago, but it wus serius mater. How could yu make light of it?" What happened? How could they make light of it?

1. *In our favorite movie, Capt. Bob marries several couples at sea. In one scene, however, he says, "If those two won't separate, I'll have them thrown overboard!" Who or what were those two?*

Answer: "Those two" were sodium (Na) and chlorine (Cl), the atoms making up the common substance we call salt (NaCl). When some of the ship's drinking supply became contaminated with sea water (which contains a lot of NaCl!), he had the drinking supply thrown overboard since the sea water couldn't be separated from the drinking water.

Concept: Solids and liquids are made of small particles that stick together. Atoms of sodium and chlorine combine to make molecules of salt (NaCl). Sea water is a solution in which salt is a solute and water is the solvent. Salt water is not drinkable.

2. *They would have nothing to do with each other until a slippery character came along. Identify all three.*

Answer: The three were water and oil, which do not ordinarily mix, and soap. When soap (a slippery character) is added, it allows the water and oil to mix.

Concept: Substances can be distinguished by their interactions with other substances. Oil will mix with other oily substances but not with water. Some substances have properties allowing them to interact with both groups. Soap is an example: when added to oil and water, it allows the two to mix.

3. *After going from third base to home, he didn't score and was very blue. Who or what was he?*

Answer: He was a plant extract (litmus, an extract of lichen) used to distinguish an acid from a base. After testing the third base with the same litmus paper, the paper became very blue; the experimenter then took it home.

Concept: Several substances may seem different and yet react in similar ways: acidic substances turn certain plant extracts (such as lichen) red; basic substances turn the same extract blue. As litmus paper reaches saturation, it becomes very blue and can no longer be used to determine whether a substance is an acid or a base.

4. *When Zulu arrived late at the lecture hall, the professor was saying, "You can add them together in two different ways: one way results in nothing, the other results in twice as much." What was the professor talking about?*

Answer: He was talking about two forces. Differences in the directions in which two equal forces are applied make a big difference in the result. (Two equal but opposing forces cancel each other out, but two equal forces applied in the same direction have a net result of twice the force of one.)

Concept: The direction in which a force is applied is important in deciding the effect. Two forces applied in the same direction will have the same result as one force equal to the sum of the two. If the two are applied in opposite directions, the effect will be that of one force applied in the direction of the greater force but with a strength equal to the difference of the two forces; two equal but opposing forces have a net effect of 0.

5. *He frequently traveled by plane, but it never got off the ground. After getting off the plane, he remained in his seat. Why?*

Answer: He did not use an airplane; he used a ramp, or inclined plane (a simple machine), to roll his wheelchair from one level to another.

Concept: An inclined plane is a simple machine with which an object can be moved and lifted more easily.

6. *She was involved in energy conversions at the lab. She often transformed chemical energy to heat energy and then to mechanical energy, but she wouldn't tell anyone about it. Who was she?*

Answer: She was a rat. The energy conversions she was involved in were the natural processes taking place in her body.

Concept: All organisms convert chemical energy (supplied in their nourishment) to heat energy. Animals can further convert heat energy to the mechanical energy used in physical movement.

7. *They claimed to be using only solar energy, but we knew they burned coal and petroleum. How could this be?*

Answer: They knew that the ultimate source of most of the energy we use is the sun.

Concept: Coal and oil started as plants that used the energy of the sun for their existence and stored this energy through the ages. Therefore, we can say that even the energy of coal and oil are, ultimately, of solar origin.

8. *Mom was cooling the house for a party and had placed a thermometer in every room. She asked Jake how much heat remained in the sunroom, but he said he had no way to tell. Why not?*

Answer: A thermometer measures temperature, not heat. Jake's mom should have asked him the temperature.

Concept: Heat and temperature are closely related. Though heat cannot be directly measured, we can measure temperature with a thermometer (when heated, mercury expands and rises in its glass tube, allowing us to read the thermometer).

9. *Her collar had no wrinkles, but she would have to iron it or it would never be attractive. Why?*

Answer: She made refrigerator magnets and had just finished a decorative plastic "collar," but would have to glue in a small disc of magnetized iron ("iron" it) before it would stick to the refrigerator.

Concept: Materials containing iron can be magnetized.

10. *When the class needed his help, Phil resisted. The teacher put Phil at the head of the class. Why? Who or what was Phil?*

Answer: The teacher wanted to show a diagram at the front of the classroom, but it was too dark to see. Phil was a filament (coiled tungsten wire) in an incandescent light bulb. When the teacher switched on the light, the filament resisted the electric current. As a result, the wire heated up and gave off light.

Concept: Electric energy is transmitted through a conducting material. Most conductors offer some resistance to the current. Electric current passing through resistance creates heat—an often undesirable effect. In electric heaters and incandescent light bulbs, however, resistance is desired *because* it results in heat and light.

11. *Though there was no mirror, she saw her friend's reflection. Where was she looking?*

Answer: She was looking directly towards her friend and saw the light reflected from her.

Concept: All surfaces reflect light. When we look at an object (or person), what we really see is the light reflected off that object. When the light reaches the eye, the cornea and lens focus it on the retina, which sends electrical impulses to the brain through the optic nerve. The brain interprets the signals to produce the images we "see."

12. *He was so strong, he could bend a three-inch thick bar of iron. When he was asked to bend this, however, he had to call on his smaller, nearsighted friend for help. What was he asked to bend?*

Answer: He was asked to bend light; he borrowed his pal's glasses to do the job.

Concept: Lenses—including magnifying glasses, spectacles, mirrors, and even drinking glasses—are said to "bend," or refract, the light that passes through them. Refraction occurs because light waves travel at different speeds depending on the material through which they pass.

13. *He went to the store to pick up a black tie. When he got home and took it out of the bag, he exclaimed, "This isn't black, it's red!" What had happened?*

Answer: He had gotten the tie from a display that was illuminated with pure blue light. The tie had absorbed the blue light, and since there was no red light for it to reflect, the tie appeared black.

Concept: Light contains many colors mixed together. An object appears colored because it reflects more light of some colors than of others. A tie is red because it absorbs blue and green light, reflecting only red. In pure blue light, there is no red light for it to reflect; it absorbs the blue light and looks black.

14. *His pitches were perfect, with the fastest curves ever demonstrated in the ball-park. Unfortunately, his team lost the game. Why?*

Answer: He was the singer of "The Star Spangled Banner" and had perfect pitch. Since he sang in a very high key and the waveforms representing his voice were shown on a giant monitor, his notes were seen as the "fastest curves" in the stadium. Too bad the baseball pitcher for his favorite team was a dud.

Concept: The difference between high and low tones is called pitch. Higher pitch results from faster vibrations of sound waves; therefore, the sine waves representing higher pitched sounds will oscillate more rapidly (have "faster curves") than those of lower tones.

15. *In science class, a message was passed to Gerald when Ms. Grayson wasn't looking. Gerald immediately revealed the message by telling the teacher out loud, "You have a lot of nerve!" She only smiled and said, "I guess we both have nerve." Who passed the message? What was going on?*

Answer: A nerve cell in Gerald's ear passed him the message. Ms. Grayson had just asked the science class to explain how she was able to hear sounds; Gerald was answering her question.

Concept: A student such as Gerald can hear the teacher's question because the vibrating air next to his ear causes his eardrum to vibrate, which in turn stimulates nerve cells to transmit electrical impulses to the brain. This gives him the sensation of sound, and he is able to hear the question. By Gerald's response, he meant that Ms. Grayson was able to hear because of her nerve cells. (Note that his response is only part of the reason we hear sounds.)

16. *He had no working navigational panel and was as blind as a bat, but he made a perfect landing. How did he navigate?*

Answer: He was a bat; he used sound to navigate.

Concept: Bats send out high-pitched sounds which echo off surrounding objects and return to them, letting them know where everything is located.

17. *Gina and Juan each parachuted from a different plane at the same time. Though they fell in parallel lines, they became closer together as they approached the ground. Why?*

Answer: They were on opposite sides of the earth, and gravity pulled them each closer to the center of the earth.

Concept: The earth's gravity pulls objects towards its center.

18. *It stretched out its long tail in the sun and soon disappeared. What was it?*

Answer: It was a comet.

Concept: Comets are small bodies that travel around the sun and are largely made of ice and other materials. When a comet goes near the sun, it forms a long stream of vapor we call a tail.

19. *Theresa was eating her own pie quietly when Geo suddenly pushed the plate aside violently and made a mess of both their crusts. She knew Geo was under a lot of stress, but why the violence? Who or what was Geo?*

Answer: Geo was the earth. Pressures built up where two crustal plates slipped past each other. The result was an earthquake, which not only altered the earth's crust, but messed up Theresa's pie when it fell to the floor.

Concept: The earth's crust is divided into large plates which float on a less rigid layer below. The plates sometimes slip past each other or away from each other, or one may move over or under the other. Where plates move against each other, pressure may build until it is released by means of a sudden movement or fracturing within the crust (an earthquake).

20. *The bank deposit turned out to be a solid investment. Later, it became a liquid asset. What was the investment? What was the liquid asset?*

Answer: The initial investment was sediment deposited on a river bank. The sediment turned to rock and, later, to molten (melted) material.

Concept: Over years, sediment can become compressed into rock. Rock can become buried due to various geological events; under high temperatures and pressures (due to volcanic activity, for example), rock can become molten.

21. *It was only a poor rural area, but Rio took up a collection and somehow pulled contributions out of the air. Who or what was Rio? What were the contributions?*

Answer: Rio was the river, which was collecting water (the contributions). The water came from precipitation.

Concept: Precipitation comes from water vapor condensed in clouds and provides a source of fresh water to the land. Some of the precipitation collects in waterways, such as rivers.

22. *Hernandez wanted to put all the pieces of the puzzle back together, but Drifty had spread them out; now they seemed to be stuck. Who or what was Drifty, and what was the puzzle?*

Answer: Drifty was continental drift. The puzzle pieces were the continents; the original puzzle was Pangaea.

Concept: Around 200 million years ago,

the land was probably all connected. We call that original continental land mass Pangaea. Pangaea is thought to have broken apart through movement we call continental drift, creating the continents we know today.

23. *By running in circles at one location, X caused a collision hundreds of miles away at another location. What is the collision? Who or what is X?*

Answer: X is circulating ocean water, which affects air temperature and creates weather patterns. One result is collisions of warm and cool air masses over land.

Concept: The earth's rotation causes ocean water to circulate. The ocean temperatures affect the overlying air temperatures, which create weather patterns when moving over land. Air masses of different temperatures sometimes collide and cause changes in weather.

24. *The children were huddled together for warmth, but Jake said, "When they spread out, we'll feel warmer and circulation will improve." What was he talking about?*

Answer: Jake was talking to the kids about the air molecules. Jake knew that when the air heated up, it would expand (the molecules would spread out), making the air lighter and causing it to rise. When the air cooled again, it would descend. This cycle would result in increased air circulation.

Concept: Warm air is less dense because the molecules of warm air are moving faster and bouncing off one another, causing them to spread out. Cold air is denser and stays low, pushing the warm air up. As air rises, it cools and then descends again; it is this cycling that drives the winds.

25. *Shirley complained to the jail warden that she needed a kitchenette in her cell. "I*

demand equal treatment. Rosa has every necessity and can even make food right in the cell!" Why is Rosa special?*

Answer: Rosa (the genus name of roses) is a green plant at the correctional facility. The plant gets light, water, and air; with these ingredients, the plant is able to make its own food right in its plant cells.

Concept: Green plants use photosynthesis to create food. After taking in carbon dioxide (CO_2), sunlight, water (H_2O), and various nutrients from the soil, the plant cells make oxygen and sugars to feed the plant.

26. *Sal refused the turkey, and Dan was embarrassed because he hadn't known that she was a vegetarian. A friend said, "You should have taken a closer look at her mouth." Why did he say that?*

Answer: Sal was a cow, which is a herbivore (vegetarian). By looking in her mouth, Dan would have seen the broad molars adapted for grinding grass instead of tearing meat.

Concept: Plant-eating animals usually have molars that are broad and flat for mashing plants, while meat eaters have long, pointed canines for tearing flesh.

27. *He was one of the most successful warriors in all the kingdoms. He had overcome much of the neighboring kingdom, but he could never force the subjects into his own kingdom. Who was he? Why couldn't he bring the subjects into his kingdom?*

Answer: "He" was humankind; humans are part of the animal kingdom. He was trying to conquer the plant kingdom, but a plant can never be part of the animal kingdom.

Concept: Living things include the kingdoms fungi, plants, and animals, as well as one-celled life forms.

28. *They failed to adhere to regulation when they allowed excessive production at the factories; therefore, they were executed. Who or what were they? Who executed them?*

Answer: They were cells in the body. (Cells can be thought of as factories producing new cells by division.) These cells were cancer cells, which didn't adhere to regulating factors governing cell division and divided too frequently. They were killed by radiation therapy.

Concept: Certain environmental factors govern the cell cycle by signaling the appropriate time for division. When cancer cells are detected, they may be killed by chemotherapy or radiation therapy.

29. *Breaking the code will allow him access to the family fortune. Though he will inherit plenty of gold and silver, he may never be rich. Who is he? What is the code, and what is the inheritance?*

Answer: He is an unborn child who will "break" and carry out the genetic code in his cell nuclei. The genetic material passed to him will ensure that he has hair of "gold" and that it will eventually turn to "silver," though he may never have much money.

Concept: To a large extent, our physical features are determined by heredity. Each parent contributes genetic material, which is stored in cell nuclei.

30. *Although they left detailed clues as to their whereabouts, the best detectives could never take them alive. Who or what were they?*

Answer: They were past life forms who had left clues in the form of fossils.

Concept: Over time, life has evolved into many forms. Today's life forms represent a small proportion of all forms known to have lived. We know this by studying the records left by fossils.

31. *She was chained down and eaten by her food. What was going on?*

Answer: While living, she was at the top of the food chain and ate other plants and animals lower on the chain. When she died, she was "chained down," or put at the bottom of the food chain, where lower plants and animals made use of the nutrients from her decomposing body.

Concept: Energy is transferred up the food chain as animals eat plants and then are themselves eaten by other animals. Energy is transferred back to the bottom of the chain when organisms die and decompose, and nutrients are recycled.

32. *In the physics club, they had made fun of his spelling. Later, he wrote, "It happened a long time ago, but it wus serius mater. How could yu make light of it?" What happened? How could they make light of it?*

Answer: The event was the fusion of hydrogen atoms in a star (in this case, a particular star called Sirius). They could interpret what they saw as light ("make light of serius mater") because their eyes were capable of sensing the light waves and sending the signal through their optic nerve to the brain. Since the star Sirius is nine light-years away, the light they see is actually nine years old.

Concepts: In a star, hydrogen fuses into helium, resulting in energy that radiates out as light. The distance traveled by light in a year is called a light-year; the light we see from stars very far away has traveled many light-years (at present, the star may even be burned out!). In a human, the cornea and lens focus light on the retina; nerve cells pass electrical impulses to the brain through the optic nerve so that we finally interpret the impulses as light.